Starborn Paperbacks

Alex Barr moved from Manchester to a smallholding in Pembroke-shire in 1996. The move has inspired much of his later work. The poems in this collection have appeared in leading poetry magazines in the UK, USA, Ireland, and Canada. In 2000 he won third prizes in both the National Poetry Competition and the Peterloo Poetry Competition. His first collection, Letting in the Carnival, was published by Peterloo in 1984.

He was born in Manchester and educated at Manchester Grammar School. After seven years in journalism in various cities, he studied at Portsmouth Polytechnic and was awarded a Diploma in Architecture with distinction in 1972. Most of his subsequent career was as a senior lecturer in the Art & Design Faculty at Manchester Polytechnic (now MMU). He is married to Rosemarie, a ceramic artist.

Also by Alex Barr

LETTING IN THE CARNIVAL

Alex Barr

HENRY'S BRIDGE

Poems

Starborn Books

HENRY'S BRIDGE
Alex Barr

First published in 2006
by Starborn Books
www.starbornbooks.co.uk

The right of Alex Barr to be identified as the author of this work has
been asserted in accordance with the Copyright Designs and Patent
Acts 1998.

ISBN   1 899530 27 4

Contents

Here	13
Another Fronrhydd November	14
Towards Pen Caer	16
Land Adjoining	18
Mathry	19
Horizon	21
Dark Matter	22
Waiting For You To Come Home	24
This Is The Shell She Found	25
Dream In The Style Of Magritte	26
Single-Sex School	27
Home To Roost	28
The Author Adduces 12 Reasons...	29
Night On Ithaca	30
Homage To Dolgopolski	32
Great Uncle Charlie's *Golden Treasury*	33
After You've Gone	34
The Invention of The Wheel Comes Of Age	35
Manufactured Friends	36
Half Moon Ride	37
Dark Iron	39
Bedding Plants For My Father	41
Large As Life	42
Our Lady Of Paris	43
How I Passed An Hour	44
Ynys Meicel	45
At The Southernmost Point	49
Henry's Bridge	50
All Change	52
Somehow I Envy Them	54
Universal Judgment	55
Llanelli Beach	57
White-Out	58

Smoke Of The Earth   59
In The End   61
Steel Stair, Haverfordwest   63
Worms   71
Death Of A Black Cat   73
Drake   74
Harmonious   75
If Only A Sheep   76
Hilary Hahn At The Proms   77
The Allegri String Quartet At Fishguard Festival   79
Before The Recital   80

***

Grateful acknowledgment is made to the editors of publications in which these poems first appeared:

Agenda: 'Death of a Black Cat'
The Antigonish Review: 'White-out', 'Large As Life'
Apalachee Review: 'Our Lady of Paris'
Grain: 'Universal Judgment', 'After You've Gone'
Peterloo Poets Prize Anthology 2000: 'Bedding Plants for 'my Father'
Peterloo Poets Prize Anthology 2003: 'Single Sex School'
Poetry Wales: 'Another Fronrhydd November', 'Dark Matter', 'Dream in the Style of Magritte', 'Homage to Dolgopolski', 'Ynys Meicel', 'At The Southernmost Point', 'Henry's Bridge', 'Smoke of the Earth'
Rattapallax: 'Harmonious'
Reactions: 'Hilary Hahn at the Proms', 'Night on Ithaca'
The Rialto: 'Home to Roost' (as 'Begin')
Scintilla: 'Llanelli Beach'
The Shop: 'Manufactured Friends' (as 'Artificial Friends')
Smiths Knoll: 'In The End'
Stand (new series 1999): 'The Allegri String Quartet at Fishguard Festival'

'Land Adjoining' won third prize in the National Poetry Competition 2000 and appeared in *The Independent* and *Poetry Review*

For Rosemarie, James and Laura

HERE

Not with the weight of great events
but bearing the slow fall of tiny actions
that thicken like the needles under larches
the strange place tilts towards the idea of home.

ANOTHER FRONRHYDD NOVEMBER

After Laforgue

Sod great thoughts with a draught around your ankles.
The house is a gallery of cobwebs and outside
the wind's playing bowls with the plastic chairs
tormenting the yellow broom.

Winter's coming, winter's coming back.
Wind howls in keyholes
a horn, a sad horn of autumn
an organ sound, the vox desolationem.

The drenched shitty-arsed sheep, nose upwind
huddle against the barn with its holed cement-wash roof
another year hasn't mended, dreaming of summer grass
in manky coats that'll soon be green with algae.

Where's the harvest now? Rolled in plastic.
The wind dishonours the corpses of hollyhocks.
Sod the land sod the garden sod the rain.
Somebody hug me please.

John's grid thing for grabbing hay bales
is rusting. His trailer's rusting.
Tractors bugger the sodden fields to ruts.
Where are the suns in farming calendar photos?

The organ note, the vox desolationem . . .
Clouds rush in hard from the Irish Sea,
apple and pear trees writhe at their stakes,
ducks lose dignity, feathers blown to blazes.

The sun rolls grudgingly along the fron
like an egg dropped in dirt
and dies messily behind Letterston. Come back!
We're damned till another spring.

All right winter, then get on with it--
make your severe revisions to my garden
while I lie sleepless. Oh congratulations,
take away everything, not just the leaves,

tear down the overhead electric wires,
anathematise the phone lines
after you've sung a funeral anthem through them . . .
and the double diapason through the keyholes.

It's a change of tone all right.
King Catarrh says forget the shade of ash trees.
Oh yes, we all know what's coming.
Count the logs, make more tea,

pull your chair so close to the stove it singes,
stare at the iron box of red events
coffin of all the suns.
Sod the rain sod the land sod the garden.

This is it every year. Every year
I'll hug the fire, hold on to tea and bread,
music, a little hope
and with these annals trash the name of winter.

Towards Pen Caer

Dead weather
 dead weather

sky rinsed out
 land rinsed out
  colours all run
   to nowhere

except, on the torn skyline
 the blotted blues
  of the subtle glazes
   on old Chinese vases

except, on the pleat of ridge
 before the skyline hills
  the ash-turquoise hues
   of scented smoke

except, on the pleat of ridge
 before that ridge
  a blush of lavender like
   the breast of some rare dove

except, on the nearest ridge,
 a sampler of green
  leaf acid sage
   viridian bottle jade
    in bands and patches

and the lizard tone of trees
  and the cottages white
    salmon, coral, parchment

delicate weather
  weaver's weather
    dyer's weather.

Land Adjoining

Badly you want it I can see. *Duw* yes. Your eyes
are hungry for these great block gateposts and
my side of the shared hedgebank with its crisscross
mysteries of shade and unreachable spaces.

What can you offer? You will have to tempt me
with more than that. Forget what *I* paid for it.
Would a man sever part of a good handkerchief
lightly? Would he retreat from his frontier easily?

When I regard you sidelong with my hooded eyes
you do not see the fight in them. Small domains
have swallowed enough men with healthier bones than ours.
This six-metre strip could bury an infantry platoon.

Yes yes, that is a better offer. But still I hear
your heart beat with desire for the hot pride of having
this long view from your barn conversion windows:
the sun rising over my lush coming grass.

Badly you want it. Good. Think of what you will conquer.
A sixteenth of an acre of pasture. A few timbers.
A useful sheet of iron. Two sycamores, an ash
in full, no longer shared. A rustling hawthorn thicket.

A family of reed buntings. A nest of wrens.
Beetles of many breeds. Ten thousand spiders. Access
to your barn's eastern eaves. A handy new opening
to your lane. (Isn't a wide gate a sight to die for?)

The air above will belong to you, not to mention also
that sharp upside-down pyramid of shale, magma,
nickel-iron and so on all the long way down.
No, I won't take less than the price of a whole acre.

MATHRY

At dusk your fairy lights entice me from your summit.
Like a song from *Bluebeard's Castle* or *Kismet*
about a treasure heap of glittering precious stones
you fill me with the desire to hurry forth at once
       keen to *be* there.

Your hill swells into the narrow crimson band
of sunset sky lying under a most profound
blackness. Random stars are a foil for your symmetry.
In this half empty land you seem a sanctuary:
       oh to be there.

So I ride out now, leaving my lonely farmhouse,
and soon you're as near as Mars viewed from Deimos,
the sun lighting each dear little rectangle of wall
(or triangle), tidily arranged on the curve of hill,
       and I'm going to be there.

               *

      I cycle up Bryn Amlwg
      looking for the village heart.
      Is it the tall grey church?
      Is it the chug-chug
      of a Mansel Davies 30-tonner
      idling at an empty corner?
      Is it the rough patch
      of green? Or the dark
      form of this iron lamppost--
      one of the lights that first
      drew me away from home?

      Home! That far-off shaving
      of pink wall, and violet

smudge of barn in mist, in folds
of strange field and wood,
    so hard to see there.

HORIZON

After Emerson

The air outside is delicious,
there are things to do, a roof to mend, and yet
here I am thinking of Eason, Owen,
(shall I go on?) Hawkins, Mackle, Thomas,
Robins, Barham, Vaughan (John Wesley's friend),
Owen ap Dafydd, who all
assumed this property belonged to them,
chose paper with bell-like flowers for the north bedroom,
took physic from that slim bottle we dug up,
saw blood-red clouds above Carn Llidi,
whose daughters dawdled along our lane
admiring (shall I name them?)
primroses, campions, yellow celandines,
whose carts made ruts like miniature canals,
who bid for old steel rails and built new barns,
subtracted acres, 'added brook to pond'--
when all the time the place was going to be ours:
mine, up here with a pad,
and hers, doing something complicated downstairs.

So Fraser, Summers, Jilani (to postulate a few),
keep your dogs off our lawns, keep the lawns neatly cut,
fell as many sycamores as you like
but spare the poplars, willows, and ash we planted
and especially spare the cherry.
That blue on the henhouse door we rather like
is Johnstone's 'Horizon' eggshell lustre--
use the same to repaint it.
The midsummer sunset behind Garn Fawr? Ours too.

DARK MATTER

'I don't *know*,' I murmured
among drying terry nappies
in the Crouch End flat
where Kennedy was murdered,
under the great ceiling rose
that took a whole tin of paint,
when you asked unhappily
after we put the light out,
'Do you love me?'

    'I don't know what love *is*,'
I answered and felt
the space between us empty.
I would have told you more
last night as you settled
to sleep, your crinkled eyelids
closed, the familiar angle of black lashes,
the cover hiding your cheek
under its blue stars. But shyness,
not wanting to wake you, held me back.

    Today at dusk
you drove to a meeting saying,
'Back for dinner before I go out again.'
A month ago we still enjoyed
pink-and-gold sunsets at seven.
Now the sky disappears at six.
Where are you? Are you not hungry?
The pasta is sludge, the boiling water lava.
Your voice would calm the thud of the clock.

    On TV news there are floods,
a malign glimmer of lakes.
A girl cries, her precious books awash,

and I rush without a torch into
the greedy lampless murk.
No small white car in the yard.
No flourish of headlights where
the lane curves out of sight.
No sound of an engine, only
a downpour beating tin.

I have been afraid of this
vertigo of the heart,
vigil in inky rain,
everything swallowed up except
the dull bulk of the barn,
the outline of a hedgebank,
the black flames of trees.

Nothing can help me now.
Not even what I have known
for years and failed to tell you
before you fell asleep:
what binds this holding
to the heavens, and keeps the heavens
from flying apart forever
is the secret, even pull of the dark matter
hidden among the stars.

WAITING FOR YOU TO COME HOME

Remember the first time
I opened my door to you?
Long before that, when

the Great Bear was over the wood
when I trod the seaweed
on Llanfairfechan beach

when Martin showed me
a snapped-off blade grown deep
into the furrows of an oak

when I sang in the gang-show
These are the times
you will dream about

you existed somewhere
and though I imagined you
I never imagined *You.*

A moment ago I noticed
blue and yellow ribs of sky
framed in a window feathered

with flying seeds caught on cobwebs.
And now? Another moment
moored in silence

a rusty honey extractor
a loaf without an end
a handful of dates.

THIS IS THE SHELL SHE FOUND

that day on the beach at Tenby
grey tinged with amber
worn saucer shape
drilled by seaworms
ridged, faintly rayed
pale souvenir of tides.

Here on the black earth
of a flower tub among
thin chrysanthemum stems
just as she must have placed it, it's
a moon in a night sky
tugging the seas
of blood in the hollows of my heart.

Dream In The Style Of Magritte

A lawn. A youngish man
a youngish woman
some way apart, kneeling.

She crinkles her oval face
as if in a sandstorm
tugs at her russet hair.
He hunches, big hands
placed as if protecting
his cropped head from hail.

The sun bursts
through altocumulus
and throws on the grass
the violet shade
of a white glider
a tree height above.

The open cockpit's empty.
An unseen source
produces a thread of incense
which curls to vertical.

The glider isn't moving.

In the silence
one shadow wingtip
touches the woman
the other touches the man.

Each is unaware
that overhead
the impossible is occurring.

SINGLE SEX SCHOOL

Kavanagh claimed that Errol Flynn
had a penis thick as a rolling-pin
and twice as long. With gasps and sighs
Leigh flung chalk dust onto his flies
as if he'd come. McKay and Mather
lying on two desks pushed together
mimed a couple engaged in sex.
Nunn started a newspaper: *The Durex
Daily*. Owen asked us to measure
our engorged instruments of pleasure
for a survey. Girls didn't interest Priddey:
'My sole delight is in my own body.'
Quartermaine splashed from head to toe
that photo of Marilyn Monroe
with seminal fluid. One lunchtime, rowing
with sea-cadets (In! Out!) Ricks and Ronan
I stole the oars from a skiff of girls.
Their pale wet hands, their alien coils
of hair over collars of black-and-gold
blazers, their excited anger, turned
my blood to lava. On the cold
waters of Platt Field Lake, I burned.

HOME TO ROOST

You were my pretty ones?
I hatched and reared

you with the twisted beak
the shape of pincers,

you with the draggled bib
stained with red breakfast?

So I should know
your grizzled baldness, Flinteye,

your rearward stare, Screwneck?
I see you are home to roost.

The potatoes are blighted
the time of the peach is over

even the spiny cacti
are mere puckered pouches. Nevertheless

I will feed you all. Begin.

THE AUTHOR ADDUCES 12 REASONS FOR LIKENING HIMSELF TO GERMANY

One. He found the Romans tedious.

Two. He kicked the Church in the backside.

Three. He wasn't sure of his boundaries.

Four. He invented names for dogs.

Five. Give him the land where lemons bloom.

Six. He was fragmented into many states.

Seven. By the time he got himself together
             conquests were out of fashion.

Eight. There is a time he speaks of
             only to warn the young.
             Did he listen to the still
             mountain and forest voices
             of real mastery? No.
             He listened to a loud harangue
             that said *Be the Cock of Europe.*

Nine. Today's economy is strained
             with structural problems
             but hopeful signs.

Ten. He'd like it known
             he won't have corruption.

Eleven. He's discovering
             his role in the world.

Twelve. He's no longer
             divided against himself.

Night On Ithaca

'The name SORRENTO (Sirentium in antiquity,
Surriento in dialect) derives from Homer's tale
of the bewitching sirens.' --Tourist leaflet

He writhes in the warm dark
in tight winds of sheet
shakes my bed
a ripe chrysalis
aching to burst.

I free him. His wrists
are ridged and welted.
'You have explained
your other wounds
not these.'

He moves to the window.
Parched hands on shutters.
We beat along the cliffs
and then--Sirentium!
I start to understand.

That sapphire sea
fiery with flecks of light
lurching through arches of tufa--
His grey eyes
are old with water.

Ropes hugged my wrists.
The mast smooth to my skin
warm to my arching back
flag high at its truck
jerking and jerking

30

sky streaming cirrus
and song--
He turns to the night sky
the dark roads of the sea.
I stand behind him.

Look at me. Tall. Warm.
Hair loose, loose--

Go. Torn' a Surriento.

HOMAGE TO DOLGOPOLSKI

Begin by looking at the empty paper
around this poem (like the water
around Tenochtitlán), rest your eye
in its whiteness, test it with your fingernail
or teeth. If one or two lice or teardrops
land there, will they not appear
like proto-words, protests of women and men
against the ancient inner silence?

                                        If you go
through this poem again, read aloud,
feel the words on your tongue.
I may be dead, my name and who I was
forgotten, as whoever first made words
from air is forgotten--even so
I hoped I would make some movement in your heart.

NOTE: A.B.Dolgopolski studied 140 languages of Europe and Asia and listed the 15 words that appeared most representative of the original proto-language. In order of decreasing stability, they are: I, two, you, who, tongue, name, eye, heart, tooth, not, fingernail, louse, teardrop, water, dead.

GREAT UNCLE CHARLIE'S *GOLDEN TREASURY*

Here in the book you bought
    And signed a century ago
Some of the pages are still uncut.
    I'll slice them now.
Here's Rossetti's 'Sudden Light':

I have been here before,
    But when or how I cannot tell:
I know the grass beyond the door,
    The sweet keen smell . . .
Lines that in fifty years you never saw.

Oh armchairs. Oh collar--stiff.
    Oh voice--reedy, refined, wary.
Oh Great-Aunt's corsets creaking if
    Life was too literary.
Oh oil of macassar massacring your quiff.

After You've Gone

Once again I tidy
the toys you scrambled for when you arrived.
The two narrow beds you slept in
are hard to reach across the litter of
a beseiging army of tiny men. Their hands
are clips designed for holding
swords, ramrods, banners with heraldry,
laser guns. I rattle them and their matériel--
jetpacks, a green chair, a small black pig--
into the crude wooden bus I made you
out of an offcut. All aboard--
you're leaving again for Shelf-land.

Now I can get in close enough to strip
the bedding to bare duvet,
autumn shades of mattress.
The pillows are still dented where you slept
satisified after we read you stories
of heroes old and modern. I love these signs
of your separate lives, the smell of your hair and skin.
Under the pillows two beseigers,
a knight with a helmet Dürer might draw,
a pirate captain without his plastic hair--
the favourites. Loved while you were here
they reach out with stiff arms
and empy hands designed for holding.

THE INVENTION OF THE WHEEL COMES OF AGE

That dashing Italian pram, *Giordano,*
rode high across the Heath
on the chrome of its undercarriage.

The superstructure, finished
in blinding white luxury plastic,
reflected the brilliance of spring.

Honeycombed in blanket
your round little features peered
from under the shell-shaped hood,

your charcoal eyes drinking
the parade of blue and treetops,
the amazing arriving world.

MANUFACTURED FRIENDS

A screw I'm using rolls
head first into a crack.
There are a hundred more
but I can't leave this one lost
like someone stuck in a well
so struggle to get it back
and suddenly
I'm four years old among
the features of my manufactured friends.

Dark haunting eyes
of a horn two hole button,
neat ears of an Art Deco vase,
gob-struck mouth
of a standing pewter ashtray,
fresh face of the boxwood wheel
Mother missed for pastry,
belly-button and ballet legs
of the dancing scissor-tongs.

HALF MOON RIDE

Two twenty-seven, light rain falling, a little heat
from the hedgebanks. A hard slow pedal uphill
to mail your card. A charming finger-post
from the days when you were a girl
tempts me with black iron letters on white wood
to Crockernwell . . . but mine has to be the road
across the bridge (a stone one you'd approve of)
and the brown racing river.

By the black pump that reigns
over the village square I post
the damp card with its bland words, then freewheel
back to the snug half-hidden house
with the Flash and Sifta salt
and someone saying, 'We've got an hour, it's four.'

Always at four
you put away the brush and Brasso and went
upstairs. I waited for your transformation
from Mrs Mopp into a movie star.
Down you came down in a cloud of eau-de-cologne
with a painted Mona Lisa mouth
and drank tea from a cup
with a scalloped rim, because in those days
mugs were enamel, for bus-drivers and soldiers.

Your card will have left its red box by now.
I should have written Thank You
for those cosy afternoons with rain outside
(the radio playing the overture from *Carmen*,
or 'Enjoy Yourself, It's Later Than You Think')
and thanked you for much more, on a long roll of card
posted like a prayer-wheel before you die.

You'd like this room, the rain
diving off the eaves, the tabby asleep on cushions.
Enjoy yourself.

DARK IRON

(for Alex Barr, foreman joiner, 1882-1972)

Late in life, Granddad
I'm trying to use your plane
a dense baulk of timber
seventeen inches long.

Punched into it
are two short names:
yours on the flat front,
your father's in the throat
from days I can't imagine.

I'm using it badly.
It pitches. It wallows.
Judders along this door edge like
a launch in a thumping sea.
Floods of rough pine
fill the mouth.

I curse. I kick.
Your granddaughter-in-law
comes to see what sullies
the fine spring air.
'How do I set,' I fume,
'this bastard of a blade?'

She fingers the superstructure
the high arabesque of handle
the dark iron before it
burred by blows
remembers her woodwork lessons:
'Tap the wooden wedge
then the blade--calmly.'

Tapping slowly
in small adjustments
I lose myself. Soon
through the throat
pour silver waves of shavings.

The door edge is level
a long shining loch
your plane travels over
in racing trim.

Your name on the nose
is my name.

BEDDING PLANTS FOR MY FATHER

The daily *vierge* the Sun King deflowered
wasn't an individual to him
but pattern-fodder, like these ageratums
Mum says must be formal.

My heart resists. My heart is Japanese,
prefers the brush-stroke to the ruler's line.
Symmetry is a graveyard.

'We're doing it for your Dad,' she says. I see him
up in the cloud rack squinting past his thumb:
Blue, five inches, blue, five inches, white.

The little plants aren't eager to conform,
their stems not centred on their rootballs.
I heave one half an inch sideways in the soil.

Mum tells me Dad loved these ritual rows
because my Granddad worked for the Duke of H---
whose gardener was his friend and taught him order.

And suddenly I remember how the Duke
had called his country home Chatellherault
and must have gardened in the French tradition.

Blue, five inches, blue, five inches, white.
This is Versailles, this is the Sun King's bed.

Large As Life

Suddenly, having entered
your presence unannounced
a person is there--

all of them, heart, liver, spleen,
hair, eyes, polished fingernails.
Nothing is left to imagine.

In my dream I called you to dinner.
You came! I was amazed
how richly you laughed.

You had booked a journey
'through the Water Board,' surprised
such things could be done.

The steep road leads home
under the dark trees you christened
The Wood of Small Misdemeanours.

When a person is no longer
arms, voice, black springs of hair
everything is left to imagine.

OUR LADY OF PARIS

'It's a grasshopper, Notre Dame,'
my Serbian friend insisted.
'When you are there you think
flying buttresses are legs.'
In the morning sun your mother and I
sat in the little square
to the east, where the Seine divides
and the buttresses *were* legs--
while you, daisy-faced in a white sun-hat,
gazed up from your blue pushchair
at the huge thing hulking against the sky.

Twenty-eight years later
my Serbian friend is dead.
There is no-one I can complain to
that the buttresses are just buttresses,
that Notre Dame never left the Quay of Flowers
to sing in harvest fields, that its empty armour
blocks the sunset as your mother and I
sit in the little square, dwarfed as ants,
dazed as ants who lose
their eggs in a scalding flood. The past
has altered. I see it as it was, too late.
Too late even then, even though
you were so small and warm
and humorous, alive, our lady of Paris.

How I Passed An Hour

A young ash had grown
too close to the lane.

One hand on the smooth bark
I sawed the narrow trunk

then sliced little branches off
to leave a ragged staff

I let fall on the earth.
I think it was your length.

The rest I burned. The black
buds were about to open.

YNYS MEICEL

1

Yes, I will come, you said.
We left the car on the clifftop
and ran down to cross
the lean strip of steel
over the numbing drop
between aprons of rock.

Far below, an amber sea
veined with ivory foam
thrashed its tail in the narrows.
No other way to reach
the white tower on the island.
Feet on the deck like thunder.

2

Aggression of wind and rain.
Sky the colour of armour.
I am driving towards the mist
and there it is, the ghost
of a lighthouse, far off.
The land is insubstantial.

The wind tries to hurl me
back in the car, but no,
I will not be pushed, although
I know what I will find
as I butt my way to the bridge
and the battering khaki sea.

3

We rushed over the bridge
then up by a stout wall
shipshape against grass
with muted embroidery
of simple plants. How many
steps? Too quick to count . . .

Already close to the white
encrusted desert buildings
under the round tower.
Men looked out through windows
cut as if into icing
to see what we wanted there.

4

I soar from the heights down
to the drawbridge barred
by the Malachite Portal
whose seven locks each
have seven levers, each
seven curlicues of brass.

But I have been conversing
on the Circle of Thirty Slates
with the Hidden Ones, who gave me
seven words to remember,
seven keys not to lose.
Yes, yes, I am coming.

5

I have run down to the great
grid of aluminium gate
with its sunburst of spikes,
a diagram made real
by the skill of Head Wrightson
years before you were born.

I cannot grip to shake it.
The bars are wired away
from all but my finger-ends.
I would make the smooth padlock
leap on its torc of brass,
burst the cold hinges.

6

Down the basalt steps,
hands on the red rail,
we rushed acrosss the bridge
then up the emerald bank
with its ribbon of blue-grey wall
and mounted Ynys Meicel.

A hundred and fifty feet
above the gold sea the light
beat like a stainless heart.
A bronze arrow vane
pointed the way to Ireland
across Carreg Onnen Bay.

Yes, I will come, you said
we will all live together:
Mother, you, the children.

The wind took away your words.
Men peered from windows
to see what we wanted there.

AT THE SOUTHERNMOST POINT

I watch the palm-trees fold their tattered prayer-books
and silently retract into the sunstruck lawn.
The statue by the pool takes her gaze
off the limp David, her companion,
puts her clothes back on, and drifts away.
The butterfly-orange all-American
rotary-engined biplane makes its final approach.
The butterflies fold back into their cases

and the hollow voices begin,
distant though not with radio distance,
coming and coming as the sea goes down,
(the blue breaking into what I should have known
blue really is) and now on the south horizon
a mud-wave, a living tide.

I wait at this extremity
the former shore of Bone Island. Stumble
ahead of the rest, suck-footed, or in your coating
of cold and slime I will not know you.
Under the widening circles
of the last frigate bird
I wait for you to ask
again, 'Are we nearly there yet?'
and for your embrace of earth and water
to simplify our equation
to nothing equals nothing.

HENRY'S BRIDGE

The river: slow between levees
whose grass is rubbed by soles
and rutted by cycle wheels.
The wind is a voice in power lines
(what does it say?)

A day like any other?
No, you have come unbidden
to walk. I have left my work
willingly, willingly
(set that down).

River of absent fish
surveyed by a slumped heron.
Your eyes play guessing games.
We step over lumps of iron
(smoothed by time).

How do places move us?
What do you mean to do?
What do you mean by silence?
How are you, oh how are you?
(I want to ask).

Clouds like ink in water.
Grass rubbed by soles.
Bare trees in drifts, rectangular towers.
Golfers in perfect pullovers on green
(across the water).

The sun muddles through
and now: Simon's Bridge

Donated by Henry Simon.
'Not Henry's Bridge?' you ask
(amused by its green girders).

Now shall we return
along the slow river
forever disappearing
ahead into the bend?
(Many have passed this way.)

You will catch a bus? Yes,
a bus. Will it bring you back?
Will you buy a return?
The clouds are ink in water
(your hair is black).

How do places colour
the crossthreads of our work?
How do we deal with them?
How do we set them down?
('It depends,' you say.)

Goodbye, goodbye in the sun
where once a stone trough stood
mentioned in a book
stuffed with our city
(oh, what was it called?)

What could I say to you
apart from another question?
The sky was vitreous blue.
A day like any other?
(willingly, willingly).

All Change

Little fires for the dead!
Three banks of night-lights
on black steel shelves lined with foil.
Red uncials on a card on the bronze
grille of the Lady Chapel
affirm *Lighting a candle is a prayer.*

Your granny and I are here
to try to illuminate
the night you blundered into.
The lights are in tiny cans
the heaven blue of Our Lady's robe.
None have been left for us.

But there are marvels yet . . .
The cathedral shop manageress
speaks on her mobile
into the void and brings the verger:
a verger purged of joy or the gift
of tongues, who brusquely gathers
the burnt-out offerings in a plastic tub
which once held olive margarine.

We long for the shy white wicks
of his new lights, but no:
first he must move all existing flames
up to the top shelf, two deep
in close-packed array
like shining souls promoted
from the Heaven of Good-looking Gods
to the Heaven of Unsurpassed Gods.

He ignores the candlelit impatience
on your granny's face, and my

grim smile as he whips his hand
away from the blazing heavens.
At last, in a cardboard tray
far below the racks of radiance
in the pattern of a honeycomb
he places the pure unlit.

Your granny teases up
(delicately between finger and thumb)
a small waxen stalk.
We light your lamp from someone else's.

SOMEHOW I ENVY THEM

--the women who wash the steps
of pale grey marble
under the scented void
of the dome of Il Redentore
on Giudecca the thin thin island.

If I could bring the candles
in cream-coloured bundles
shine the silver
change the cloths
on the altar of Il Rendentore,

if I could place fresh flowers
in tall heavy vases
under the scented void
of the dome of Il Redentore
I would cling to nothing, no
not even belief
or the astonishing purple of the roses.

UNIVERSAL JUDGMENT
13th-century mosaic in the Basilica, Torcello

What was I meant to do
to be led through those flowers
I don't know the name of
with gold lustre leaves and Byzantine petals?

How could I have joined
the little balding men
with beady eyes in the queue
to be lifted onto the holy Knees of Jesus?

Gabriel and Peter
are showing a diagram:
in a tall rectangular frame
flowing with blue and white
between pairs of eye-patterned wings
a head on a disc of gold.

Whose head and why?
Whose bare feet under the wings?
Whose hand holding a slender staff
crowned with a bobbin? Gabriel
(he too has a slender staff
crowned with a bobbin) eyes me
sadly as if to say *Come ON!*

Against a golden sky
with tall feather-duster trees
Mary holds up her palms

meaning *Forget it.*
Next to her in a loincloth
holding up one palm
(a cane cross in the other hand)
is John the Baptist. *Sorry,*
too late to dip you now.

LLANELLI BEACH

You have to begin with this road
and the dead curve of sand
reached under a sign about renewal

on which there is a picture
in generous pastel colours
of people playing under trees

of which there are few at present.
You have to begin with this
like the man in the blue tracksuit

teaching his son to fly a kite
which will not perform, which leaps
and wiggles from side to side

with a background of the Gower
and wolf coloured water
then drops by an empty tube

of industrial lubricant
on the dead curve of sand.
You have to begin with that.

WHITE-OUT

Forward into the white-out
a fat new notebook
no map no compass
no life or landmark

no wren in a battered birch
no rock with a face's shape
only to the end
grey lines a tide of fences.

Forward writing what?
The cat sleeps on the sill?
The car is packed and ready
for the far end of the land?

Forward to the flame
or pressed campions
or sky of tears for which
the last page is waiting.

SMOKE OF THE EARTH

Actuary, actuary
mathematical visionary
state in clear vocabulary
how far is it to the door of Death?

Using trigonometary
actuary, actuary
show me x tabularly
(x = distance to door of Death).

I'm aweary, a-weee-ary
a state that's neither temporary
nor so extraordinary
so--how far to the door of Death?

Surely my poor urinary
tract, spasmodic mesentery
make me fodder for the mortuary,
bring me in sight of the door of Death?

Classicist, classicist, what's that river
that sets your balls and bowels a-quiver,
chills your mind and heart and liver--?
Oh, I thought you pronounced it 'Leth'.

Missionary, missionary,
ears still wet from the seminary
play me a Christian-military
march as I slog to General Death

among the common fumitory
lit by the lesser luminary

till, when my soles are scari-
fied, still far from the door of Death,

lift me astride your dromedary
missionary, missionary--
gallop along the hard and hairy
piste to the *porte* of M. Death.

Wary, wary, yes, look wary,
in that I may choose to vary
the contract by an arbitrary
stroke and *summon* Mr Death:

put the little treasure through his paces
out from his door in shirt and braces
tripping over his undone laces
narked and knackered and out of breath.

Huckleberry, Huckleberry
build me a raft of Styx for a ferry
I'll sail in like Commodore Perry
and stick my foot in the door of Death.

Hey, you double-acts--Tom & Jerry,
Smith & Jones, Two Ronnies, Eri-
c & Ernie--you'll be transitory
alongside BONES (that's me) & DEATH

soon to appear at *The Cemetery*--
No! A grave mistake! Don't bury
me but burn me, reliquary
urn me inside the door of Death.

On the ground
snug and sound
sound as a pound
parked in peace on the floor of Death.

IN THE END

Remember in *Kidnapped*
Ebenezer?
Grim miser
face like ash
cheeks like craters
downdragging mouth
eyes on swivels
weighing up nephew David
trying to do him in.

I was David.
In forty-seven
they gave me *Kidnapped*
Told in Pictures--
brilliant pictures
by Dudley D. Watkins
of Desperate Dan fame.

I was shipwrecked
fought in the roundhouse
fled through the heather
quarrelled with Alan
won his friendship
and in the end
ousted Ebenezer.

I was David
until today
fifty years on
when in the mirror
cheeks like craters

downdragging mouth
a face like ash
swivels its eyes.

Ebenezer's back.

STEEL STAIR, HAVERFORDWEST

CELEBRANT: There's an air on the stair.
                We'd call it expectation
                this crowd and I
                if we had any expectation.
                Maybe a flight of doves
                from Isola San Michele
                wheeling north-west
                will settle there
                a wing-blizzard high on the stair.

                Three flights ascend
                in line towards
                the arrow of a gable,
                three half-landings
                on slender columns
                of brick wound with ivy,
                and like a scaffold
                a great steel balcony
                at the stairhead.

CHORUS: Buggered old town
                all around
                handful of swans
                concreted Cleddau
                NatWest shoe box
                legendary Argos
                ill-fitting Boots.

CELEBRANT: We stand at noon
                my bride at my side
                the crowd around
                under knackered backs
                (High Street, Dark Street)

tall and Georgian
slate grey, render grey.
High behind us
old stone prison
unloved castle
flags down for Margaret
no *son* and *peu de lumière*.

CHORUS:

Drained old town:
Moravian memories
Regency facades
Thomas's Green
all drain down
to sad Castle Square
with its boarded Abbey National,
bouquet of sizzling onions.

CELEBRANT:

Into the air
go the long steel rails
of the red and green stair
to union with the balcony
the great steel scaffold
under the gable's arrow.
A stir.
At the stairhead a stir.
Something eclipses
low-voltage lights
behind French doors.
whose glass flashes.
*Que les portes
soient ouvertes--*
let the doors be opened!

CLOWN:

In come I, Clown--

MAGICIAN:

In come I, Magician

through the Clown
and down
leading by a rod to the head
(her skull as high
as my thigh)
a figure in a wedding gown.

CLOWN:
In come I, Clown
in odd socks and bands
of white and blue.
The *real* Clown. My ghost
was a theatre trick
reflecting the work
of old Professor Pepper.
And I hurry down,
past the Magician
with the Skeleton Bride
hollow-eyed,
for whom I open
on the highest half-landing
with a gesture that's pure
an imaginary door.
Nyissad ki még a két ajtót--
let the door be opened!
Creating an air
down we all come
descending the stair
under which you stand
your bride at your side.

CHORUS:
Drained old town
all drained down
leaving its two dark churches
like macaws chained to ancient perches.

QUEEN: In come I, Queen of Cups.
Diamanté heart-shaped clips
hold my grey hair back
from a centre parting,
in my right hand the biscuit tin
embossed 'East West Home's Best'.
Agorwch hi . . .
yes, let it be opened,
let the inside of its lid reflect the skies
or mirror my deep-set eyes
and faded rose-petal skin.
A fresh-cut *Rosa Mundi*
is in my left hand. The crowd
who were never loud
fall silent
under the castle
as my ankle-booted feet
move as if to the beat
of an unheard drum.
Down I come.

CHORUS: And all around
the buggered old town
thrusts out its districts
each severed from the other.
each restricted
by railway, bypass, river.

ALCHEMIST: Attention! In come I, Condottiere
tight-lipped, heavy-eyebrowed, weary
from the campaign
but I do not complain
though my legs are not my own.
Each of us is alone
with his thoughts.
Retorts?

Yes. Neck of a retort in either fist,
down come I, Alchemist.
Apere ostium! (Apere os tuum!)
But now, standing
on the highest landing
I take my greatcoat off
like Colline at the end of
La Bohème, broad and stern.
My legs are my own!
I seek you in the crowd
who shuffle and stare
awed by my air
and cowed
as I descend the stair.
Yes I, Philosopher,
of few words and fewer embraces
will find you among the faces.

CHORUS: Knackered backs . . .
and high behind us
the unloved castle
the old stone prison.

GOOSE GIRL: In come I, Goose Girl--
unsteady. I almost fall.
At the head of the stair
I blink at the overcast
like a hostage free at last.
My long fingers feel
for the reassuring steel
of the balustrade, and slowly
down I come,
in my free hand a fat sack.
Are my slender neck
and long black braid
familiar? Are you afraid?

Am I the Princess or
the Impostor? Will I fall?
How frozen you stand
side by side
you and your bride
under the stair
down which I come
with such an air.

CHORUS: All around
the dishonoured town
falls silent
and the hush on us, the crowd
who were never loud
under the wasted castle
grows deeper
as the five
(are they alive?)
go on descending
to the lowest landing.

CELEBRANT: And now I am at the edge
(somehow)
of the crowd
no longer at the side
of my bride
foot on the first tread
of the steel stair
the green and red
I cling to the balustrade
whose uprights alternate
straight, wavy, straight
as the five on the lowest landing
whisper, extending
hands, *Come, come.*

My feet are lead
I am on the second tread,
the third . . . then standing
with them on the lowest landing.
All five embrace me
even the Alchemist
their embraces
fumes, cobwebs, dew,
sea-fret, cloud-shadow.
The stair
takes on the air
of a celebration.
As if working a mangle
the Magician turns the handle
of a pipe-organ built of birch.
A fairground sound:

ORGAN: *wheep-a-whipple-whipple*
              wheep-a-thump-thump

CELEBRANT: The Clown mimes
              how I should mount the stair
              high into the air
              the Alchemist shows me drawings
              of the intermediate landings
              the Goose Girl and Queen of Cups
              take my arms gently--*Up!*--
              a*s* the magician turns:

ORGAN: *Thump-tatter-tatter-wheep-wheep*

CELEBRANT: Up to the head of the stair!
              They whisper that there
               in low-voltage light behind
              the glass of the French doors
              that open from the great

steel balcony
is the *Imperatrice* Sarama-Gula
waiting for me, waiting
on black silk pillows
her beautiful dogs around her.

Now I am looking down
on the raggedy old town
which isn't quite so buggered
which perhaps has its charm.
The crowd stare up at me
silent, shocked, afraid
and down there is my bride
the true *Imperatrice*, pale
her eyes black pinholes . . .
By the Five I am led
across the steel scaffold
towards the French doors.
The Goose Girl draws
from her sack a cloak of feathers
for me to wear
and all around
(goodbye grey old town)
and all around is air.

WORMS

Let's get this into the open.
Your gone-off peach, aubergine, and carrot
have puckered like struck marquees
then run to slime, and you have this vision
of us moving in, which is why
you say our name with a curl of the upper lip.

But it's not just that. No, it's this other picture:
your loved one underground, the amazing wiring
of median and intercostal nerves gone
to mash, the hamstrings of the thighs
frayed to barbs like a rusty hulk's hawsers,
the Islets of Langerhans, every gland,
slumped into elements . . . And us
reaming the dear flesh, bringing it
into the dreadful light. Don't the crumbs
of rich silt that cling
to our sunrise-coloured skins comfort you?
Why do our uncoiling dances make you squirm?
We're just decommissioners, death-technicians.

When we make a point we follow it up.
Our tunnels are beneficial--we air the subject
you'd rather keep sealed.
We're vessels of newly coined
soluble phosphorus,
exchangeable potassium.

Whatever you think, the stuff
we carry up in our bodies
isn't the same, isn't the same at all

as the glutinous liquescent matter
that catches you out in dreams.
We'll keep on trucking it up into the sun.

DEATH OF A BLACK CAT

He clipped fur off your foreleg--
you would no longer need it.
I stroked you. He flicked the hypodermic.
You panted into the final straight.

Now I shave the sweet grass with a hook,
strip the turf, hack out the ochre earth
among young apple trees, and think
of the easy kitten days--

lingering Sunday mornings when the children
still full of dreams dazzled the garden room
with talk and music. You lie
curled in your basket, eyes not shut entirely,

white of a tooth showing. Soon
this flat slate marker will be hidden
and I'll forget exactly where your grave is.
You'll have the glimmerings of ubiquity

wherever the long sward will grow.

DRAKE

Walking, you're a white baggy clown.
Standing, a strange machine that tilts to observe the sky.
Making love, you and your partner look like
the last seconds of a dirty water-polo game.

You puke black mud into clean drinking-water.
In any language--*qua-qua, coin-coin*--you sound like a fool.
You're immortalised by bath toys, umbrella-handles,
and Daffy and Donald the famous fall-guys.

And yet just now in a rainstorm
that turned the chickens to heads of mops
and me, with my hair plastered to my head,
to the villain of a melodrama

you and your partner strolled around like owners
and for one fine moment
up you reared, chest out, wings extended,
formal, white, heroically heraldic.

HARMONIOUS

Little snail, your yellow shell is fragile
and you are not agile:
how does your heart abide with danger?

'To my world you are a stranger.
Until I am poisoned, pecked, or crushed
my days are harmonious and unrushed.

'I move with muscular rhythm like a lover.
So high, the heads of golden grasses hover.
Between their trunks run fabulous plated beasts.

'Green lace adorns my feasts.
My shining path is a clematis tendril.
The frames of climbing beans are my cathedral.'

If Only a Sheep

stood still on a concert platform
and didn't search the stalls for grass

if you lifted its back to look inside
and saw hammers instead of chops

if it knew more than a single note
and how many bleats to the baa

if its wool had gold lettering *Steinway*
instead of *W* daubed in blue

then with its rows of ivories
its neat black legs

bearing its noble weight
it would be a grand piano.

HILARY HAHN AT THE PROMS

I never let the violin out of sight
she says in the TV interview.
It's like having a kid.

How tender she is, how very
fierce as she feeds it notes,
an eagle tearing prey,

hair flaring back as if in wind.
The bow bobs and thrusts
at the demanding strings.

Now we cut to a flock
of greying first violins.
whose gaunt faces mask

what? Sympathetic joy?
Rapture? Envy?
(Her youth! Her altitude!)

Or the emptiness of ageing?
Close-up: Hilary's highlit fiddle.
How sleekly *it* has aged.

And the players who passed it on?
There--just out of shot.
A long phantom line

reaching back to the maker
weighing up the wood
of maple, Swiss pine, willow

andante in a forest
into whose canopy
a mating warbler is weaving music.

THE ALLEGRI STRING QUARTET
AT FISHGUARD FESTIVAL

If we invent the world as they say
each of us a solitary source
how bold of me to make this music.

I created these four performers
washed their creamy jackets with brilliance
directed their elbows' lambada.

From the muddy well of my own heart
sprang the thought that at the touch
of rosined hair strings would cry aloud.

No Guarnerius curved a belly
No Schubert dotted a quaver
I remain the sole fountainhead.

Those evaporations of myself
now return as not-myself, as rain
slakes a land that had forgotten water.

BEFORE THE RECITAL
St David's Cathedral

High in the double zigzags,
carved in the pale stone
of great leaning arches,
ancient shadows
from the season of the sea-god
gather at heads of columns,
along the little arcade
of the triforium,
in every boss and bracket
of unpainted oak
under the plane of ceiling.

Ahead, our view
of choir galleries, high altar,
shrine of the saint, is blocked
by the masonry of a rood screen,
with John, Jesus, Peter
as wistful figureheads.
Above them, with carving
as intricate as seaweed,
an oak balustrade like
the rail of the open bridge of a ship.
Above that, ah
the superstructure,
the great bank of sirens,
the organ.

> *Swell to great,*
> *choir to great.*

Distributed here
too far apart to touch
(unless we slide along

these pews whose polish drowns
reflections of tiny arc-lamps)
we wait for the recital.

Hidden mechanisms
lie oiled and ready,
trim little ventilators open
mouths in expectation.
We watch the bridge
its polished horizontals,
the shining verticals of the sirens.
Will they sound
signalling the departure
that may alter everything?
This is the hour in port when
the last boxes hang from the sky
loading, ours among them,
and black tugs crouch
like genuflecting clerics.
When at bollards on the empty quay
those manning ropes await
the captain's orders.
We watch the bridge--
is he on his way?

> *Swell sub-octave,*
> *tremulant.*

No. The sirens
are silent. There are no
ropes to unreel.
This nave will never sail
exposing the shrine,
baring to the wind the bones of Dewi Sant.
There is only
the silence we wait in

under the lead roof,
the sea unheard
half a mile away.
Beyond the windows
the last lumens die.
Even here in the west
we cannot hold the light.

Great to pedal,
swell to pedal.

Insulated in
our clothing, we wait.
Silent as birds
in a night forest, shadows
roost in the lozenges
and beads of the blanched arches,
between the tiny arc-lamps,
around the unstained windows
of the outer wall
beyond the furthest pew,
under the chancel arch, and
(as if in a hedge of poplars)
between the pipes of the organ.
The shadows cluster
in unseen groves above the choir,
where hollow fallen trunks
(some overgrown with tracery,
some serpentine like old apple branches)
and thickets within thickets
of tiny and tinier tubes
(delicate straws, elf-cups,
fungi the shape of ears)
wait, as we wait
for wind, for the breath of life.

Choir to pedal,
tremulant.

Or so we imagine. But
the visible organ pipes
are lifeless palings,
fake flues that never sound.
The hymn-board has no numbers
the columns and arches
are stripped of colour.
Into the silence weave
memories of other arches
other darkness
other organs,
cries of unseen sheep
the shuffle of a foot
the dead-leaf rustle of a programme
the boom of a door closing.

Claribel flute,
koppel flute,
sesquialtera,
ophicleide.

We are too far apart
to touch and there is
                nothing
a light comes on
            tiny
              yellow
steel shade
        a drooping buttercup
above the balustrade
        beside
  the dead row of poplars
a nest of brilliance

like light on a ship's bridge
in the void of night
close to the roof of stars.

Is somebody there?
Is it the man in tails
a white gleam at his throat?
Is the little yellow light
lighting his music?
Will he unstop the stops,
duplicate with his toes, engage
the reversible trombone piston?
Will he swell to great?
Will he play
the quiet meditations of Dupré,
sound the rich, earthy
opening of 'Bryn Myrddin'?
Will a Pachelbel chaconne
build unexpected levels
of simple throaty tones
above the cold floor?
Will the *double diapason*
give our marrow a frisson?
Will he improvise on
the deep reassuring
fluty *lieblich bourdon*?
Will we hear
the *voix céleste* creating
strange pulsations,
the *nazard*'s hollow vessel,
the *larigot*'s high whistle
never heard alone,
always an overtone?

We wait, quietly.
Quietness fills

the air to the roof
and beyond the roof
and the sea, and also down
into our breathing,
into our bones, and now
there is no space between us
we who are few
or between us and the sea.
In the silence
the dead stakes
in our hearts take root
in the memory of other darkness,
the memory of other organs.
Pilgrims without motion,
pilgrims toward music
we sit in our nests of brilliance
upright or bent
like ancient apple branches,
distributed
in this refuge of stone
that is neither ship nor forest.
We sit in the void of night
that may alter everything
in the silence that is the lever of the wind.

Tromba,
clarion,
gemshorn,
lieblich gedeckt.